Supporting
Family Literacy & Lifelong
Learning

Ontario

Culture
Ministry of

The Honourable Caroline Di Cocco,
Minister of Culture
announces Literacy Grant
through Ontario Government under
Premier Dalton McGuinty

Enhancing the vital role of Ontario's libraries
as community hubs of literacy and learning

How Does It Work?

SPORTS TECHNOLOGY

**Linda Bruce,
John Hilvert, and
Alan Hilvert-Bruce**

Smart Apple Media

This edition first published in 2006 in the United States of America by Smart Apple Media.

Smart Apple Media
2140 Howard Drive West
North Mankato
Minnesota 56003

First published in 2005 by
MACMILLAN EDUCATION AUSTRALIA PTY LTD
627 Chapel Street, South Yarra, Australia 3141

Visit our Web site at www.macmillan.com.au

Associated companies and representatives throughout the world.

Library of Congress Cataloging-in-Publication Data

Bruce, Linda, 1953-
   Sports technology / by Linda Bruce, John Hilvert, Alan Hilvert-Bruce.
     p. cm. – (How does it work?)
   Includes index.
   ISBN-13: 978-1-58340-794-3 (lg. print : hc : alk. paper)
   1. Sports—Technological innovations—Juvenile literature. I. Hilvert, John. II. Hilvert-Bruce, Alan.
   III. Title. IV. Series.

GV745.B78 2006
688.7'6—dc22

2005046773

Edited by Anna Fern
Text and cover design by Modern Art Production Group
Illustrations by Andrew Louey
Photo research by Legend Images

Printed in USA

Acknowledgments
The author and publishers are grateful to the following for permission to reproduce copyright material:

Cover photo: Skateboarder, courtesy of FairfaxPhotos/Dallas Kilponen.

Rob Cruse Photography, pp. 13, 19, 23, 25, 26; FairfaxPhotos/Dallas Kilponen, pp. 1, 16; Istockphoto.com, pp. 15, 17; By permission from Microsoft Corporation ©, p. 29; Photodisc, pp. 7, 18, 22; Photolibrary.com, pp. 5, 14, 27, 30; Photos.com, pp. 4, 24; Reuters, pp. 6, 8, 9, 12, 20, 21; Sport the Library, pp. 10, 11.

Contents

Glossary words

When a word is printed in **bold**, you can look up its meaning in the Glossary on page 31.

What is technology?

Technology helps us to do things. Technology is also about how things work. Since ancient times, people have been interested in how things work, and how they can improve technology to meet their needs. They use their experience, knowledge, and ideas to invent new ways of doing things.

The *How Does It Work?* series features the design and technology of machines that are part of our daily lives. This includes:
- the purpose of the technology and its design
- where it is used
- how it is used
- materials it is made from
- how it works
- future developments

Technology has changed the way we live in many ways. It will keep on bringing change, as people constantly invent new ways of doing things using new materials.

Sports technology, such as special clothing and shoes, can make playing sport more enjoyable.

Sports technology

During the last 100 years, technology has revolutionized all aspects of sport, including sports equipment, training, and sports coverage by the media.

Sports equipment was once made from natural materials, such as wood, leather, and rubber. It is now usually made from lighter, stronger, synthetic materials, such as plastic, **carbon fiber**, neoprene, and **aluminum**. Training methods have made sports training a science and new technologies, such as **infrared light** timers and touch pads, are being used in competition sports.

Games and the skill with which they are played are increasing in diversity and complexity, and sport and fitness have become a major part of our society. International communication networks broadcast sports into our homes and across the world. Sport-**simulation** computer games allow us to pit our wits against the computer. By using the Internet, we can play virtual sport with people in other parts of the world.

This book takes an inside look at different kinds of sports technology. It also previews some amazing new inventions in sports technology that you might use in the future.

Sports technology can be used to assess the fitness levels of athletes.

5

Tennis rackets

A tennis racket is used to hit a tennis ball. New technology in tennis rackets can improve players' performance by increasing the force with which players can hit the ball.

Where used?

Tennis players use rackets while training and competing. Tennis rackets are used everywhere people play tennis.

How used?

The player holds the racket in one hand and uses it to hit the tennis ball. Players hit the ball in various ways to make it spin and to place it in different parts of their opponent's court. To suit different players, rackets are made in different sizes and weights.

Materials

The frames of tennis rackets for everyday use are often made from stiff, light, strong materials, such as **fiberglass**, glass-reinforced polyester, steel, aluminum, graphite, titanium, and carbon fiber. Originally, strings were made from animal gut. Today, strings are made from synthetic material which is stronger, stretchier, and less likely to break.

Carbon-fiber rackets are very light to hold, and give players a stronger swing.

How tennis rackets work

Tennis rackets are designed to give players power and control. Strings that stretch more give more power. Strings that stretch less give more control. Lightweight rackets can be swung faster and provide more power. Heavy rackets transmit less shock to the player's hand, and increase control.

handle
Rackets with heavier handles give more control, because they are easier to swing.

beam
The beam size is the width of the racket. A larger beam makes the racket stiffer and increases its power.

strings
The material and thickness of the strings determine how much they stretch, and how much power or control the racket has. The stringing pattern and tension also affect force and ball movement.

head
A longer head provides more power. A wider head gives more control. Rackets with more weight in the head than in the handle provide more power because more weight goes behind the hit.

grip

What's next?

In the future, tennis rackets will be more closely tailored to the height, weight, arm-length, strength, and age of the player. This will make tennis easier to play and give players more control over the ball.

Timers

A timer is used to measure how long an athlete takes to perform a task. Timers can include touch pads, **digital** photography and video, and infrared and **laser** light beams.

Where used?

Individuals wishing to improve their performance use timers. In competitions, automatic timers are used to measure how long each competitor takes, and to determine the winner.

How used?

The timer is started as soon as the task begins. When the athlete completes the task, the timer is stopped and the time recorded.

Materials

Timers are made from materials, such as metal **alloys**, plastic, and **silicon**. These are selected because they are light, long lasting, strong, and easy to shape.

In sprints, timers in starting blocks detect false starts. Digital video is used to determine race placement. Athletes also view videos to analyze their performance and plan their race strategy.

How timers work

Automatic timers work by recording the time competitors start and end the race. When the competitor triggers the touch pad, light beam, or camera at the end of their race, a signal travels to a computer, which calculates and then displays the time taken. In events, such as marathon running or bike and horse riding, competitors carry a **silicon chip**. When they cross the finish line, an infrared beam reads the code on their chip, recording their name and time.

In competition swimming, touch pads and automatic timers determine the winner.

Touch pads on the wall at the end of the pool record when each swimmer finishes the race. The touch pads send signals to a computer clock, which calculates and displays the times taken.

Touch pads on the starting blocks detect whether a competitor dives before the official start. If so, a buzzer sounds and competitors are recalled to start again.

What's next?

In the future, timers will use radio signals instead of wires to transmit results to a central computer.

Electronic goalposts

Electronic goalposts are used to record when a goal or point is scored. They help umpires to make judgements, and minimize disputes over umpire's decisions.

Where used?

Electronic goalposts may be used in games, such as soccer, and hockey.

How used?

When the ball passes a scoring area, a signal is sent to a central computer, detailing the score. This helps to back up the umpire's decision in ambiguous cases, and prevents the crowd from blaming the umpire for decisions they dislike.

Materials

Materials selected include metal alloys, which are durable and minimally affected by changing weather conditions. The computer chips are made from silicon.

Electronic goalposts send a signal to a central computer, and the score is displayed on an electronic scoreboard.

How electronic goalposts work

Electronic goalposts work by using video and infrared technology to record the ball or puck passing the goalposts. When a goal or point is scored, a signal is sent to the umpire or straight to a scoreboard.

goalposts
Miniature sensors on the cross-bar and upright poles project infrared or laser beams. This acts like an electronic sheet stretched across the entrance to the goalposts. This "sheet" records when a ball passes through it. When triggered by the ball, electronic goalposts send a signal to a computer, which records the score.

net
The net stops the ball.

What's next?

In the future, fast-moving balls, such as those used in baseball and tennis, may have electronic "tails" on them. By wearing special glasses, the crowd will be able to see the ball and the tail it leaves as it streaks past.

Bicycles

A bicycle is a popular form of transport. Riding a bicycle is faster than walking, uses less energy than many other forms of transport, makes no pollution, and is a popular form of exercise. People of all ages can easily, safely, and comfortably ride a bicycle.

Where used?

Bicycles can be ridden on bike paths, roads and tracks, and in playgrounds.

How used?

The rider straddles the bike, sits on the seat, and grasps the handlebars. They steer with the handlebars and pedal to turn the wheels and move along. To stop, they use either a back-pedal brake, or handbrakes mounted on the handlebars. Gears on a bicycle help the cyclist to go faster while using less energy.

Materials

Bicycle frames are made from metal alloys. The tires are made from rubber. Some parts may be made from aluminum, plastic, glass, and fiberglass. These materials are strong, light, inexpensive, and easy to maintain.

Competition racing bikes are built for speed, with solid wheels, **streamlined** spokes, and handlebars that slice though the wind.

How bicycles work

Bicycles are made for different purposes. Most are made to ride on bike paths and roads. Mountain bikes and BMX bikes are made to ride off-road. When the rider pushes the pedals this turns the chain-wheel, which moves the chain. The chain turns a gear, which turns the back wheel of the bike.

seat
Springs, padding, and adjustable seat height make the bicycle more comfortable.

brakes

derailleur
When you change gears with the lever on the handlebar, the derailleur moves to a different position on the freewheel. It drags the chain with it onto a different gear cog.

frame

brake lever

gear lever

handlebars

bell

hand grips

handlebar stem

brakes

front fork

tire

wheel

pedals
The pedals move the chain.

freewheel
The freewheel has five to nine gears on it. The freewheel allows riders to coast along without continuously pedaling.

chain
The chain moves the freewheel and the chain wheels, which turn the back wheel.

chain wheels
Gears on the front are called chain wheels.

What's next?

In the future, bicycles may be designed for specific lifestyles, such as electric bikes for elderly people, and bicycles with encased gears and wheels that are designed to protect clothing.

Exercise monitors

An exercise monitor is used to measure items, such as heart rate, speed, and number of strides taken. Exercise monitors help people benefit more from their exercise training program by providing measures of how their body is working.

Where used?

The person exercising straps the monitor to their wrist, or waistband. When measuring heart rate, another sensor is strapped around the chest.

How used?

People performing exercise, such as walking, running, and cycling, may use simple exercise monitors. For example, a walker may wear a pedometer to measure the number of steps they have taken. Some athletes use monitors that combine different measures. A runner may choose a monitor that measures heart rate, speed, and number of strides taken, while a cyclist may wear a simple heart-rate monitor. Sports coaches use the most comprehensive monitors to help them plan training programs.

Materials

Exercise monitors are made from plastic, polyester, and metal. These materials are chosen because they are light, sturdy, easy to shape, and because they look stylish.

Exercise monitors are worn strapped to the athlete.

How exercise monitors work

Athletes use exercise monitors to measure heart rate, blood pressure, temperature, speed, and distance traveled. They can electronically copy this information to a fitness journal on a personal computer, or insert it into training **software**.

strap
The monitor is strapped to the athlete's chest, wrist, or waist.

display monitor
The monitor displays information, such as heart rate, blood pressure, current running pace, and pace target information. Other features may include:
- **stopwatch** (to measure the time taken)
- **energy consumption** (to measure how much energy the wearer has used in calories)
- **pedometer** (to measure how many steps have been taken).

Exercise monitors are designed to be water resistant so they will not be affected by sweat or rain.

What's next?

In the future, cheaper, more durable monitors will be widely available for everyday fitness activities. For more serious athletes, monitors will offer even more detailed information, such as the measure of maximum oxygen-carrying capacity of an athlete's bloodstream.

Skateboards

A skateboard is a short board on wheels. Skateboard riders perform daredevil stunts on their customized boards.

Where used?

Skateboards are ridden wherever there is cement to roll on. Many skaters meet at special skateboard parks that have built-in street-terrain obstacles, half pipes, slopes, and vertical ramps.

How used?

The rider stands, places one foot on the board and uses the other foot to push off. Riders can crouch, squat, sit, and lie on their boards. They perform daring stunts, such as riding on the top of rails, leaping down steps, and jumping and grabbing the back of the board.

Materials

Skateboard decks are made from materials, such as carbon fiber and wood. The wheels and trucks are made of metal alloys, **nylon**, and **urethane**. These materials are chosen for their toughness, flexibility, and light weight.

Skateboards are painted with graphics, and riders add their own decorations, such as decals, graffiti, crash marks, and scarring.

How skateboards work

As well as being purchased as a complete unit, riders can individualize their boards by choosing different combinations of deck, wheels, and trucks. The trucks screw onto the deck and the wheels fit onto the trucks.

deck

The deck is made from layers of wood, such as maple, glued together with **resin**. Some boards are made from carbon fiber. This imitates wood structure, but is more durable and water-resistant. The tail and nose of the deck are curved and raised. Decks range in size and length.

surface

Plastic sealant resists water and protects the deck. Grip tape may be added to help the rider stay on the board.

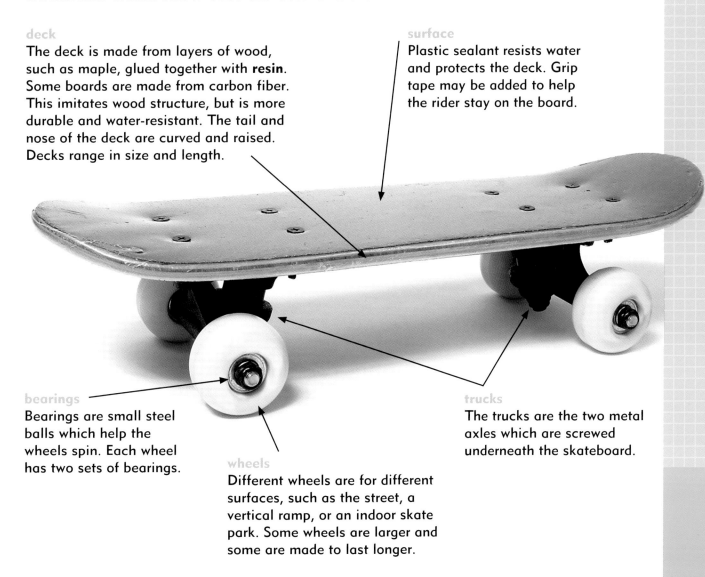

bearings

Bearings are small steel balls which help the wheels spin. Each wheel has two sets of bearings.

wheels

Different wheels are for different surfaces, such as the street, a vertical ramp, or an indoor skate park. Some wheels are larger and some are made to last longer.

trucks

The trucks are the two metal axles which are screwed underneath the skateboard.

What's next?

In the future, stronger boards will be made from new combinations of synthetic materials. New designs will make boards less likely to break and able to stop more quickly.

Ski suits

Ski suits are worn to keep people warm, dry, and comfortable while they ski.

Where used?

Because snow is freezing and wet, ordinary clothing soaks up water and makes wearers cold and uncomfortable. Many skiers wear ski suits to keep them warm and dry.

How used?

Ski suits are often worn over thin, warm shirts and leggings. The suits are designed to be worn with ski boots, gloves, and goggles.

Materials

Ski suits are made from materials, such as gore-tex, **lycra**, and polyester. These materials are chosen because they are light to wear, warm, and easy to move in. Gore-tex helps keep skiers dry and comfortable when they are exercising, by moving perspiration away from their skin. The material contains pores that lets water vapor move to the outside of the suit, while at the same time stopping water from entering. Materials with this quality are said to be able to "breathe."

Ski suits are often made of stretchy, breathable fabrics with a waterproof surface.

How ski suits work

Ski suits are made of special material to keep the the wearer warm and dry while allowing perspiration to escape.

hat
The hat protects the head and reduces heat loss.

goggles
Goggles protect eyes from sunlight and from the glare of the sunlight reflected off of snow.

jacket
A lightweight jacket with feather or synthetic filling is warm and easy to move in. Bright colors and reflective details help the skier to be seen.

pockets
Pockets have zips to stop their contents from falling out.

waterproof gloves

ski boots
Ski boots support the ankles, and hold the skis on.

What's next?

In the future, ski clothes will be made from newly developed synthetics that are even lighter, warmer, and more durable.

Body swimsuits

Body swimsuits are worn by competitive swimmers. The suits reduce drag on the swimmer, enabling them to swim faster and to shave milliseconds off their time.

Where used?

Body swimsuits are worn in competitive swimming events, especially international competitions, such as the Olympic Games.

How used?

The body suit fits tightly around the swimmer's body. Some suits leave the arms and legs bare. Others include arms and legs, and have a hood to cover the head. These leave the hands, feet, and face bare.

Materials

Bodysuits are made from light, stretchy fabrics, such as aquapel, powerflow, and spandex. These fabrics are designed to reduce the drag of water on the swimmer.

Body suits help athletes swim faster.

How bodysuits work

Full-body swimsuits are designed to increase the swimmer's speed by reducing drag and turbulence around the swimmer's body. Some suits are made from material with tiny V-shaped ridges on the surface, similar to those found on shark skin. These direct the flow of water across the swimmer's body to help them swim faster. Swim caps with a silicone outer shell and a rigid insert to prevent the cap wrinkling also help to reduce drag.

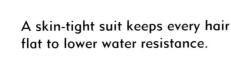

Different materials in different parts of the suit speed the flow of water across the body.

A skin-tight suit keeps every hair flat to lower water resistance.

What's next?

In the future, body swimsuits may be worn as everyday clothing. These suits may be designed to support muscles, to help prevent vibration that may slow an athlete, as well as to create a streamlined fashion look.

Athletic shoes

Athletic shoes are designed to improve the wearer's performance, prevent sport injuries, and to look stylish. Different shoes are made for different playing surfaces. Indoor shoes have softer, smoother soles that do not mark polished floors, while sprinting and golf shoes have spikes to grip the ground.

Where used?

Athletic shoes are worn both as casual wear, and when athletes are training and competing.

How used?

The shoes are slipped onto the feet and fastened with laces or velcro. Soft soles absorb impact by squeezing under pressure and returning to their usual shape. Shoes are fitted to the athlete, with designs being made for narrow and wide feet, for men and women, and with high and low cuts for different degrees of ankle support.

Materials

Athletic shoes are made from materials including leather, plastic, rubber, and metal alloys. These materials are chosen because they are light, strong, flexible, easy to care for, and minimally affected by changes in temperature and running surface.

Athletic shoes can enhance the performance of athletes.

How athletic shoes work

Athletic shoes are designed to support the wearer's feet and ankles during the specific movements the sport demands.

upper
Flexible mesh upper provides ventilation and support.

tread
The tread pattern on the sole helps to stop the athlete from slipping.

arch support
The middle section between the heel and the front of the foot, called the arch, adds rigidity to keep the athlete stable.

sole
Air units in the heel and forefoot cushion the feet.

What's next?

In the future, athletic shoes may be made from materials that do not damage the environment, and which can be recycled to make new shoes.

Helmets

Helmets make sports safer, and often more enjoyable to play, by protecting players from head injuries.

Where used?

Helmets are worn during sports, such as skateboarding, cycling, horse-riding, hockey, football, and baseball.

How used?

The player places the helmet on their head. Extra padding is stuck inside the helmet so that it fits snugly on the wearer's head. The helmet is fastened tightly with a chin strap. The helmet fits properly if it does not fall off when the player bends their head forward without the chin strap being fastened.

Materials

Helmets are made from materials, such as plastic, fiberglass, foam, and polyester webbing. The fiberglass creates a smooth outer shell. The foam softens the blow by crushing on impact. Chin straps are made from a strong material, such as polyester.

Helmets help protect the brain from being damaged.

How helmets work

Helmets reduce the chances of people being hurt, by softening the effects of knocks to the head. Some helmets have visors and face guards, to protect the face from blows and balls.

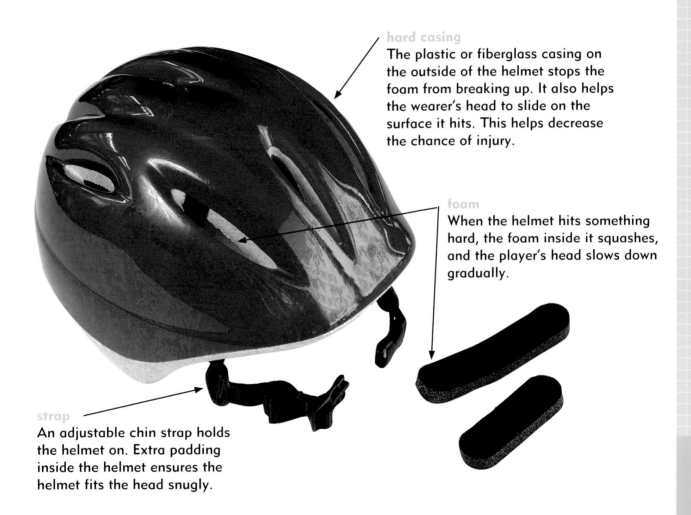

hard casing
The plastic or fiberglass casing on the outside of the helmet stops the foam from breaking up. It also helps the wearer's head to slide on the surface it hits. This helps decrease the chance of injury.

foam
When the helmet hits something hard, the foam inside it squashes, and the player's head slows down gradually.

strap
An adjustable chin strap holds the helmet on. Extra padding inside the helmet ensures the helmet fits the head snugly.

What's next?

In the future, helmets will have face masks made as part of the same mold. Helmets may also have built-in video cameras that transmit the view the rider sees to televisions screens in the stadium and Internet sites.

Televised sport

Televising sport enables more people all over the world to enjoy watching live games and replays on television.

Where used?

Fans watch live televised sport from their homes. They can also take small portable televisions to sporting events to watch televised close-ups of the event. Some venues offer televised close-ups on large screens near viewing stands.

How used?

Viewers turn on their televisions, switch to the appropriate channel, and watch the sport as it is played. For more enjoyment and closer analysis, viewers watch sport replays which include slow-motion shots of action, and scores flashed onto the television screen.

Materials

Equipment used in televising sports includes television cameras, transmission stations, and communication **satellites**. Equipment used in watching sports channels includes television sets and **receivers** which are cheap and easy to operate. This equipment is made from materials including metal alloys, silicon, glass, and plastic.

Sport is televised all over the world.

How sports are televised

First, a television camera records action and sends it to a station which broadcasts it to a satellite. Television waves travel in a straight line from their source. Communication satellites reflect them back to Earth at an angle, broadcasting them around the world.

1. A television camera records the action.

2. Video and audio signals are sent to the television station.

3. The station sends the television waves to a satellite.

4. The satellite sends the information all over the world.

5. Your television set aerial receives the signals. The image on your television is updated at the rate of 25 frames per second.

What's next?

In the future, we may watch television on TV goggles. The picture will be projected onto a pair of glasses. The sound may be heard through headphones, or a device that sends sound through your skull.

Sport simulations

Sport simulation games are computer games that imitate how the sport is played. Games, such as golf, basketball, billiards, baseball, and tennis, as well as other sporting activities, such as skiing and fishing, can be simulated.

Where used?

Professional athletes play simulation games to improve their game strategy. Fans play simpler simulations on home computers, in video arcades, on **consoles**, MPEG players, calculators, and mobile phones.

How used?

Players use a mouse, keyboard, arrows, or other input devices, to select game options, such as which golf club to use, how hard to hit the ball, and the direction in which they will aim.

Materials

Materials to make sports simulation games include metal and plastic, which are light, durable, and inexpensive. Silicon chips are used for storing large amounts of digital information in a tiny space.

Sports simulations can be used to train and teach players how to play games.

How sport simulations work

Sport simulations help players improve their game by offering players choices and showing them the effects of their actions. For example, golf simulations help players improve by displaying a course scene or problem and asking players to choose the appropriate club, and how they will adjust to wind and surface conditions. When players choose correctly, the game rewards them with a higher score.

This screen, from the start of a golf simulation game, shows where the game is being played, the weather conditions, and the golf course conditions. As the game progresses, players choose their opponent, the type of golf club they hit each shot with, the type of swing, and how much power they put into the swing.

What's next?

In the future, simulation games will allow players to play more realistically. For example, information will be sent to the game from sensors attached to a real golf club that the player swings.

How well does it work?

In this book you have read about and looked at the designs of many different technologies. As well as understanding how technology works, we also need to think about how well it works in relation to other needs, such as aesthetic, environmental, and social needs. We can judge how well the idea, product, or process works by considering questions, such as:

Manufacture	• Is the manufacture of the technology efficient in its use of energy and resources?
Usability	• Does the technology do the job it is designed to do? • Is it safe to use? • Is it easy to use?
Social impact	• Does it have any negative effects on people?
Environmental impact	• Does using the technology have any environmental effects? • Does it create noise, cause pollution, or create any waste products?
Aesthetics	• Does the design fit into its surroundings and look attractive?

Thinking about these sorts of questions can help people to invent improved ways of doing things.

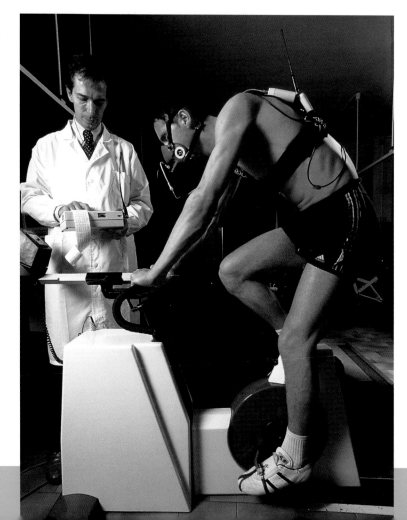

Sports technology that helps people to maximize their fitness will continue to develop into the future.

Glossary

alloys mixtures of metals

aluminum a strong, light metal which resists rust and conducts electricity and heat well

carbon fiber a strong, light material made by mixing carbon cloth and a plastic glue

consoles devices used for direct communication with a computer system

digital information stored in the form of numbers, called binary code

fiberglass a strong, light material made by weaving and gluing strings of glass together

infrared light a wavelength of electromagnetic radiation that is similar to the wavelength of red light, but which is invisible to the human eye

laser a highly focused beam of light which can produce immense heat and power when focused at close range

lycra a light, smooth, stretchy fabric made from nylon and used for sports clothes

nylon a strong, man-made fiber made from oil

receivers devices that detect radio waves

resin a type of glue made from tree-sap or plastic

satellites machines placed in orbit around Earth to perform a job, such as relaying communications signals

silicon a substance found in sand, clay, and many minerals, and used in computer chips, alloys and building materials

silicon chip a wafer-thin slice of silicon, smaller than a fingernail, which contains thousands of microscopic electronic circuits

simulation imitation of a real-world experience by a computer, such as flying an aeroplane

software a set of instructions for a computer to carry out

streamlined shaped to reduce friction

urethane tough, clear material that does not easily break

Index